a more
excellent way

a more excellent way

CHESTER A. PENNINGTON

Design and Illustrations by David Dawson

Abingdon Press   Nashville and New York

A MORE EXCELLENT WAY

Copyright © 1969 by Abingdon Press

Standard Book Number: 687-27154-1

Library of Congress Catalog Card Number: 71-86163

Scripture quotations are from the Revised Standard Version of the Bible, copyrighted 1946 and 1952 by the Division of Christian Education, National Council of Churches, and are used by permission.

PRINTED AND BOUND BY THE PARTHENON PRESS, AT
NASHVILLE, TENNESSEE, UNITED STATES OF AMERICA

TO
MOTHER
AND
DAD

If I speak in the tongues of men and of angels, but have not love, I am a noisy gong or a clanging cymbal. And if I have prophetic powers, and understand all mysteries and all knowledge, and if I have all faith, so as to remove mountains, but have not love, I am nothing. If I give away all I have, and if I deliver my body to be burned, but have not love, I gain nothing.

Love is patient and kind; love is not jealous or boastful; it is not arrogant or rude. Love does not insist on its own way; it is not irritable or resentful; it does not rejoice at wrong, but rejoices in the right. Love bears all things, believes all things, hopes all things, endures all things.

Love never ends; as for prophecy, it will pass away; as for tongues, they will cease; as for knowledge, it will pass away. For our knowledge is imperfect and our prophecy is imperfect; but when the perfect comes, the imperfect will pass away. When I was a child, I spoke like a child, I thought like a child, I reasoned like a child; when I became a man, I gave up childish ways. For now we see in a mirror dimly, but then face to face. Now I know in part; then I shall understand fully, even as I have been fully understood. So faith, hope, love abide, these three; but the greatest of these is love.

We all want to love and to be loved. And this desire is more than mere sentiment or self-interest. It is an essential human need. We sense that, if we are to live well, we must experience love.

How, then, can one be the kind of person who wins love and is capable of loving others? Everybody feels the intensity of this question—unless he turns it off. And those who have been brought up anywhere near the church know that Christianity offers a rather distinctive answer.

To achieve love is an urgent human need. To help us realize this achievement is a profound promise of the Christian faith.

THE MEANING OF LOVE

The most famous description of love is, of course, the thirteenth chapter of I Corinthians. But we are seldom content with description. We want a definition. What is love?

Interestingly enough, the New Testament never offers a formal definition of love. Instead, the authors point to a living embodiment of its meaning. It is as if these original Christians are saying to us, *If you want to know what love means, look at what God has done for us in Jesus Christ.*

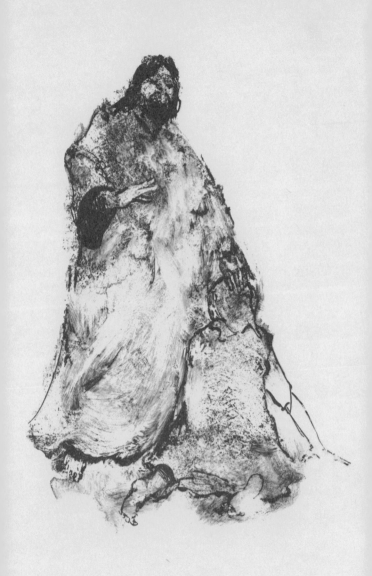

Basic to this understanding is the affirmation that "God is love." That's the way John said it (I John 4:8). Jesus had said it before, differently. God is like a father who yearns after a lovable but wayward son, and rushes out to make possible his return to the family. Indeed, God is like a father who loves his self-righteous—and therefore not very lovable—son, and goes out to him to help him act like a brother (Luke 15:11-32, esp. 21, 28).

God's love is expressed in his giving himself to us. "God so loved . . . that he gave . . . " That's the way the Fourth Evangelist expressed it (John 3:16). Jesus had said it before, differently. Criticized for keeping company with people of questionable character, Jesus quietly replied, "The Son of man came to seek and to save the lost"(Luke 19:10).

God's self-giving in Christ is the model for our relations with others.

"Let each of you look not only to his own interests, but also to the interests of others." That's the way Paul wrote it (Philippians 2:4). Jesus had said it before, differently. Love your neighbor like a Samaritan who found a man in need and couldn't ignore him, but ministered to him (Luke 10:29-37).

Perhaps the simplest way to define the love that is commanded—and celebrated —in the New Testament is to say that *love is an active concern for the good of another person*. To love is to give yourself for the sake of someone else.

But what of the emotions? Love is generally thought of as a combination of feelings. Certainly no one wants to minimize the importance of emotion. Yet the New Testament interprets love as an attitude, a way of relating and acting with other people. Feelings will vary, depending on the relationships, the persons, the circumstances involved. But the basic content of love is *the willingness to give yourself for the sake of another*. And the supreme expression of love is the way God acts for us in Jesus Christ.

LOVE IS A GIFT

There is a very important insight implicit in the Christian understanding of love. We must make it explicit and keep it clearly in mind as we read Paul's interpretation.

According to the New Testament, love is not only deed but also gift. The Christian faith is not primarily an insistent demand that we get out and love everybody. It is, first of all, a promise of God's love, and an invitation to accept his gift. Our concern for one another, then, is a response to his love. God's love is given before our love is commanded. Indeed, his gift evokes our deed. God enables us to do what he asks.

This is really the secret of Christian love. We are not expected to generate good feelings, or stir up compassion, or force ourselves to anxious obedience. Such efforts only make us more tense, more unsure of ourselves, and therefore less capable of caring about others. Rather we are invited to accept the knowledge that, always and without change, God loves us. This knowledge, deeply received, has healing and creative power. By it, we are enabled to act in loving ways toward one another.

Once again, it was John who put it most clearly: "We love, because he first loved us" (I John 4:19). Jesus had said it before, differently: You should love even your enemies, because that's the way your heavenly Father is (Matthew 5:44-45).

This is actually the context of Paul's beautiful description of love. Unfortunately, we have torn his words out of the setting in which he himself placed them. We should restore the thirteenth chapter of I Corinthians to its proper context by noting that it follows the twelfth chapter without any interruption.

In the earlier chapter, Paul is talking about "spiritual gifts," particularly as they are exercised in and through "the body of Christ." As human beings, he is arguing, we have many different abilities, which we exercise in our life together. As Christians, we regard these abilities not simply as natural endowments but as gifts of God, to be used for our common good. We are bound together in a relationship that may be compared to the corporate unity of the human body. And the spiritual gift with which each "member" is endowed is to be used in such a way as to minister to the good of all.

Now, he continues, it is perfectly proper that we should desire what might be called "the higher gifts." But there is one gift without which the others are really quite insignificant, one gift that is to be desired above all others. There is "a still more excellent way" in which we may be related to and involved with one another. It is the way of love.

Strictly speaking, Paul is writing about love as a gift of the Spirit, expressed in and through the church as the body of Christ. But I think we do not violate his meaning if we extend it to wider human relationships.

Wherever genuine love is experienced and expressed, there we may believe the Spirit of God is present and active. All true love is a gift of God. To interpret love simply in human terms is to ignore its origin. Wherever men are freed to love one another, their freedom and their love are the gifts of God. Love is more than a human achievement. It is also a divine endowment. We are enabled to perform the tasks of love as we are open to receive the gift of love.

This is the more excellent way: to know love as endowment, to receive gladly this love-enabling gift, and to live in the God-given freedom to love.

THE STYLE OF LOVE

What does love look like in our actual relations with one another? What are the attitudes that characterize love? What are the ways of acting that constitute love?

Paul introduces his interpretation of love by indicating that its absence diminishes the value of many excellent deeds. We may have splendid gifts, and may use them admirably. But unless they are animated by love, their exercise is futile, and their consequences insignificant.

If I speak in the tongues of men and of angels, but have not love, I am a noisy gong or a clanging cymbal.

And if I have prophetic powers, and understand all mysteries and all knowledge, and if I have all faith, so as to remove mountains, but have not love, I am nothing.

If I give away all I have, and if I deliver my body to be burned, but have not love, I gain nothing.

These are surely strange words. If they were not so familiar, we would be shocked by them—at least by that last one. Can it really be true? We understand that eloquence may be calculating and knowledge may be cold. But can benevolence lack compassion?

Paul indicates that it can indeed. And his insight is confirmed by contemporary psychology. What looks like generosity may be an attempt to ease one's sense of guilt. Or a man may give to benevolent causes out of conformity to community pressures. "Charity" is not necessarily an act of love.

And what if it isn't? Aren't practical needs met? Well, perhaps so. But Paul may be more right than we like to admit. Good deeds that do not express our honest attitudes may not accomplish very much. They certainly don't do anything for the doer. And they may stir up resentment in those for whom they are done—leaving us to wonder why!

We must be freed from attitudes that spoil our deeds. We must be released into genuine concern. Then what we do will say what we mean: we really care.

What does love look like? Paul's description is drawn in quick phrases, as with light strokes of the brush or pencil. It is as if he were sketching a style of life, marked by two bold strokes: accept the other person for what he is; and work actively for his good.

"Love is patient and kind"

To love other persons means to be able
to accept them as they are. Our inclina-
tion is to want them to be what we think
they ought to be. And because they are
not, we become impatient with them or
act unkindly toward them. If we could
only learn to accept them for what they
are—as, indeed, we should like to be ac-
cepted—we would learn to be patient and
kind. Maybe then we and they could increasingly become the sort of persons we
all should like to be.

"Love is not jealous or boastful"

A further aspect of accepting others is
to accept ourselves. We are who we are.
Others are who they are. Why, then,
should we be jealous of them? Or why
should we be so insecure as to try to build
ourselves up? What are we trying to
prove? Can we learn increasingly to think

of ourselves and others as equally the recipients of God's good gifts?

It is as if we are different parts of a body, with different functions. If we all had the same capabilities and performed the same roles, there would be no social organism. As it is, "to each is given the manifestation of the Spirit for the common good" (12:7).

"It is not arrogant or rude"

With increasing acceptance of one another as members of the human family, we are able to reduce our tendency to be arrogant or rude. We recognize our varying gifts and our differing roles. There is no need to be arrogant to others, as if our function were superior; or rude, as if theirs were inferior.

"The eye cannot say to the hand, 'I have no need of you,' nor again the head to the feet, 'I have no need of you.' " (12:21.) We all need each other. Arro-

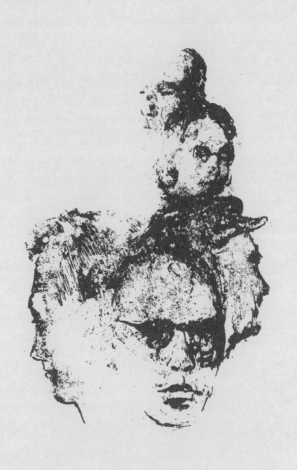

gance and rudeness spring from the failure to recognize our mutual interdependence. When we appreciate the variety of our gifts and functions, we are drawn into a sense of our common humanity.

"Love does not insist on its own way"

This is a difficult saying to understand, and even more difficult to live.

If we believe something deeply, we want it to be taken seriously. Surely, Paul can't mean that we should not be firm in our beliefs, or stand by our convictions. He was a man of rather definite ideas himself! But there is a difference between being firm in our persuasions, and trying to impose them on somebody else. Paul is probably warning strong-minded people like himself that they may become overbearing.

To love someone means to have respect for his integrity as a person. To impose my will on him is to violate this integrity, and thus really to violate love.

The tension frequently lies in the fact that if I care for someone, I want him to have what is good for him. And just as often, I may think I know what that is, even better than he does. Believing this, I may insist on my own way. But if I am sensitive to the meaning of love, I will restrain my self-assertiveness and support his integrity as a person.

There are many instances in which the actual living of this kind of respect will be difficult. What does it mean, for instance, in the relation between parents and children? Certainly there are times when parents will have to exercise the responsibility that goes with their function. But we must be careful that it is love which is motivating us, and not our pride, or fear, or self-will. We parents must learn to regard our children as real persons, and to respect their integrity.

In our relations with our peers in society, how easy it is to be insistent, domineering. We can be so sure we are right that there is no room for the other person to be himself. There will certainly be occasions when we will want to stand firm, and even insist on what we believe. But we must be sensitive to the integrity of the other persons involved, and not impose our will on theirs—not even "for their own good." We must respect their freedom to be what they believe they must be.

"It is not irritable or resentful"

It certainly is easy to be irritated at one another, and to become resentful of one another. Sometimes, of course, these reactions may be caused by fatigue or other circumstances. Husbands and wives know how easy it is to react hastily under the pressure of family tensions. But they know also that such reactions do not really contradict the genuine love that unites them. In the less personal relations of society this is not nearly so obvious. So we need to be aware that irritation and resentment are destructive. They betray lack of trust and goodwill.

It is intended "that there may be no discord in the body, but that the members may have the same care for one another" (12:25). If we learn to care for one another, and trust one another, we will be less inclined to burst out in irritation or resentment.

"It does not rejoice at wrong, but rejoices in the right"

This is one of the most searching statements of all. How often we actually hope for little things to go wrong in the lives of others, and take a certain delight at their minor misfortunes. Of course, we may never admit it out loud—not even to ourselves. We may say, "Isn't it too bad." But inwardly we may be a little glad it turned out so poorly. And at the same time we are ashamed of ourselves for harboring such unworthy feelings.

Surely, we want to be purged of this littleness. We want to have a generous spirit, so that we are genuinely glad when things go well for others. We covet an honest concern for one another, so that "if one member suffers, all suffer together; if one member is honored, all rejoice together" (12:26). We know, as a matter of practical fact, that in society the misfortune of one segment reflects on the others. Similarly, when one group prospers, many others share in their good fortune. But what we want is not just recognition of sociological fact. We want a genuine goodwill that is glad when things go well for others.

We sense that such a life style will not go out of fashion. It has a permanence that is rooted in the eternal character of God.

Varieties of human wisdom and expression come and go. But a life of the sort that is sketched in these phrases will be valued in any culture, in any age.

LOVE IS A BECOMING

We have only to look at this sketch of love with some honesty to recognize that this is not really our life style. Who can read Paul's words and say, "That's me!" We know all too well that we simply don't manage to live like that.

How, then, may we become persons capable of love? The question persists. But so does the Christian answer.

First, we must keep quietly in mind the truth that love is not only a task to be done but a gift to be received. The Christian faith does not demand that we strain

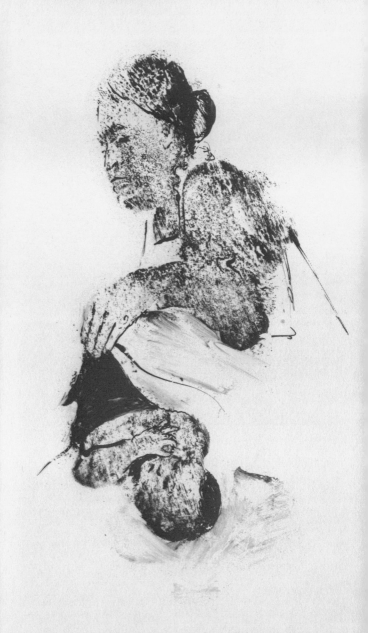

grimly to become what we cannot be. That would drive us to frustration and despair. Instead, we are invited to receive deeply into our selves the freely given love of God.

You are loved. This is the first affirmation of Christian faith.

Be open to love. This is the continuing admonition of the Christian life.

Then we are ready to understand the further insight that *love is a becoming.* Love is not a static achievement, as if we had arrived. Love is a process of growth, as if we were on the way. We should never expect to feel that we have reached the goal: I am a person full of love. That would be presumptuous. But we may expect to feel that we are growing toward the goal: I am becoming a person more and more capable of love.

This growth is really the work of God's Spirit in us, about which an entire treatise should be written. As love is his gift, so growth in love is the result of his continuing presence with us. But this can be experienced only with our consent and cooperation.

There is a sense in which love is a "gift" rather like a native talent. We say that a person with talent is "gifted." The latent ability is not something he has invented; it is given to him. It has only to be recognized and awakened. Then it must be developed by practice and discipline.

In the same way, the gift of love must be developed by practice and discipline. In order to increase his skill and improve his performance, an artist or an athlete will undertake serious disciplines appropriate to his abilities. Similarly, a Christian will follow certain practices, in order to increase his ability to love and improve the effectiveness of his life.

What are the disciplines of love? I can't count the number of times I am asked this question, nor the number of times I hesitate to answer. But I will try to answer this time—still hesitantly, and urging you to keep this reply within the context of our total understanding of love.

What would be better than to take this very sketch of love that Paul has given us, and use it as a measure of our life? Look at it periodically and ask, "Am I growing in my ability to manifest these qualities? Do I understand what may be limiting my growth? What is God trying to teach me through my family and associates? Lord, I want to be more loving."

I know a young man who did this for awhile. He had read another—and more famous—exposition of this same passage of Scripture. He listed the qualities of love —patience, kindness, and so on. And periodically he looked at them, asking, "How am I doing?"

Today—years later—he doesn't do this anymore. But he says that the verses have become deeply imbedded in his mind. And he echoes John Wesley, "I'm going on . . . ."

Increasing self-understanding is a necessary part of such growth in love. We need to know what our own particular confusions and compulsions are. Psychological insight and biblical study can illuminate each other. As we persist in both, we understand ourselves better and grow in our ability to love.

We need to have the support of a few people who accept us, who help us know ourselves, and who sustain us in our development. Hopefully, our family will do this. Associations with small groups of various kinds will surely help.

But I must return to a basic understanding. These disciplines are not undertaken as duties forced on us by anyone else, not even God. Whatever we do, we do

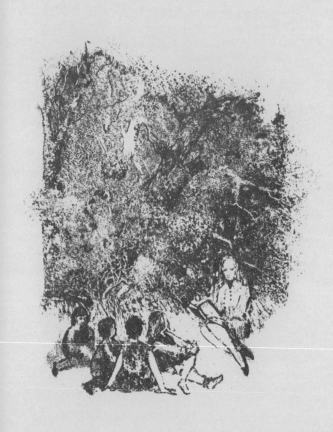

freely and gladly, in response to God's love. We try to be patient and kind, because this reflects the way God acts toward us. We want to increase our sensitivity to others, because God guarantees not only our own but also their integrity. We want to be glad when things go well for other people, because we know that in all things God is working for our common good.

Such an experience of growth is the real basis for Christian joy. We are working not to earn God's love, but because he has given us his love. We sense that the growth we are achieving is being elicited by his Spirit in us. We believe that we are becoming what God intends us to be. This is what we are created to be, and what we therefore deeply long to become.

As we grow through childhood into the skills of manhood, we increase in our ability to love.

As we see only unclearly in the reflection of a mirror, but anticipate a

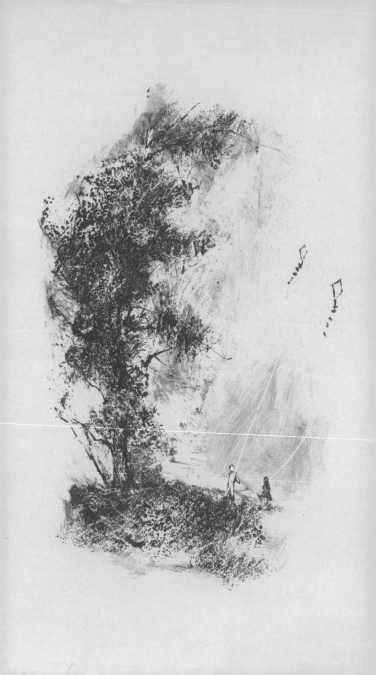

face-to-face clarity, so we hope to realize the beauty of love.

As our present knowledge is incomplete but holds the promise of fulfillment in personal understanding, so we sense that we are growing into love's fullness.

There are three enduring values in the Christian life: faith, hope, and love. But the deepest, most pervasive, most gracefull, is love.

Faith is trust in the unchanging love of God.

Hope is the expectation of love's fulfillment.

Love then—the will to seek another's good—is the greatest of all.

DESIGN AND ILLUSTRATION: *David Dawson*

TYPE: *12 pt. Benedictine leaded 3 pts.*

TYPESETTER: *Dayton Typographic Service*

MANUFACTURER: *The Parthenon Press*

PRINTING PROCESS: *offset, 2 colors*

PAPER: *60 # Carnival Offset, Putty
    Bondsanders Paper Company*

BINDING MATERIAL: Columbia Fictionette
    The Columbia Mills Incorporated